ENERGY & WEIGHT LOSS

KERRI HERMARY

www.HappyPublishing.net

ii

TABLE OF CONTENTS

INTRODUCTION

Kerri was inspired to write Energy & Weight loss with her spirit guide "Melkiezadeck," or Mel, for short, so we could educate others about the process of you becoming one within yourself through understanding the importance of energies around you!

You are two beings: an energy being and a physical being. God created the two beings to bring them together, so the spiritual plane and physical plane could come together.

God's plan is like stepping stones, and each plan gets your physical being closer to your energy being. Once there has been a connection between the two, this is when the bigger plan comes into play. But the energy being is the only being who has the wisdom of the bigger plan.

The energy being and physical being play an important part. Many humans don't know these parts or the effects of energy or how to take care of their physical beings.

It is the world around us that gives us education on how to function in the world of dense energies. These dense energies that the physical being walks through are the stepping stones to meeting their energy being.

Your physical being is developed in a light dense vibration and can't function correctly with heavy dense vibration which comes from other energy beings. Your physical being physical parts become energetically overloaded with extra weight. Humans believe they need to diet but the weight loss can only happen with energy weight loss

The physical being's body is designed to fit your energy being through a light dense vibration but is strong enough to carry extra weight. God created the physical being's body to expand, to compensate for growth. Many humans are overweight because they don't understand that the energy beings around them are making their physical being overweight through very dense vibration.

Humans resort to diets to lose weight, but this rarely works because becoming overweight doesn't start in the physical being's body. It starts in the human brain with thoughts and ends up in the physical being's body.

It is the thoughts human tell themselves and believe, that becomes excess weight. But these thoughts are just energy, a vibration. Humans don't realize thoughts and words create the physical being's body to become overweight in energy. Excess eating of food makes the physical being's body fat in the cells.

Think of a balloon. The more thought or energy you put into the balloon the bigger it gets.

Cause of Weight Gain

For example, Kerri heard over and over in her mind she was fat and once she believed her thoughts, her physical being had to obey. Her body become what she was thinking and saying in her mind. Kerri was nowhere close to being fat but believed and felt fat because her energy in her mind was fat.

Human brains don't come trained. It is the energy beings around us that train humans and then they take that information and train their brain.

When we think of an idea or thought it comes in energy form because it hasn't manifested.

Everything that we think about starts as an energy thought, but thoughts come as pictures and you can see it by visualizing it.

We will see pictures in our heads easily because we all see things daily which end up in our mind as an image or experience. Like how we picture ourselves this image is already in our energy field which manifests into our reality. So, our thought on our beliefs have been in our layers for many years.

As we put more energy towards our thoughts, things begin to manifest.

Kerri's journey of learning to listen to her energy being and retraining her thoughts has been the most rewarding schooling she has ever attended.

Kerri chose to experience this lifetime physical and mental abuse from another physical being. Over several years, Kerri's physical being was trying to communicate to her that her situation was causing the weight issues.

Thanks to her energy being's and physical being's teachings, she was taught the most important lesson: both the energy being and the physical being need to be aligned with each other so she may live a disease-free and be able to live in the present moment!

Kerri's energy being was and still is in control throughout this whole earth plane experience!

It is Kerri's intention that as you read these pages, you will learn about your own energy being and physical being and discover more joy, health, light and love in your own life now.

~Kerri Hermary and Mel

We are all energy beings! We are all one!
God created us in his image.

Each human has two beings: one, the energy being which is the real you, the unseen, unsmellable, and untouchable you and contains the energy systems; and two the physical being, which contains the human physical body that is your vehicle on this planetary visit.

Energy beings and physical being are parts of God's universal energy of intelligence.

Each part is independently and uniquely designed to complement each other. Energy beings have a very high vibration of wisdom that is always connected to God.

Energy beings communicate intuitively through Clairvoyance, Clairaudience, Clairsentience and Clair cognizance.

Clairvoyance means "clear seeing" and it is the gift to see spirit forms which are seen in the mind's eye (spiritual eye).

Clairaudience means "clear hearing" and it is the gift of hearing spirit voices or noises which are heard inside the head (spiritual ears) or as external sounds.

Clairsentience means "clear feeling" is the gift of feeling others' emotions or physical energy. Gut instinct falls into this gift.

Clair cognizance means "clear knowing" is the gift of knowing stuff without being told.

The real you is very intelligent and knows everything that you require to communicate with higher vibrations of knowledge.

God's universal energy is full of ancient wisdom about you as an energy being. It is not the physical being that carries from life to life, it will be shed off when the physical experience comes to an end.

For each new adventure a new physical being is designed to fit that vibration. Humans need to understand that the physical being is just temporary, here while your energy being experiences what they need do on this earth plane.

Your energy being has total control throughout this experience and the physical being's only job is to house and carry your energy being during this earthly experience.

Humans always ask: What is my purpose? The human's only purpose is to carry your energy being and enjoy the experience. All humans go through the same stepping stones but at different times. All humans are equal, but it is their mind that makes them different.

Humans are all looking for the magical pill to a successful experience. Humans: there is no pill!

God created two complex beings to come together while experiencing God's other beautiful planes.

There is no magical pill!

Your energy being is capable of travelling outside your physical being while on the earth plane. Your energy being can see your physical being's every move and future. When God created energy beings, they were a duplicate of God's energy of love and light.

You have always been a perfect energy being from creation.

Your physical being is very intelligent as well. God designed each part to work hand in hand. The different is your physical being can't communicate to higher vibrations without your energy being.

The physical being was designed to be able to communicate to lower dense vibrations through seeing, hearing, smelling and touching.

Most energy beings aren't sure what to expect when they choose to enter the physical realm.

Along their journey, humans begin to understand their purpose through this travel to earth. Kerri has been on this journey of understanding her own physical being. Over the years of trial and error, she has come to realize she doesn't control her physical being. It is her energy being "driving," which lays within her physical being.

All energy beings are pure loving light and we all come from one source, God, the universal energy which surrounds each one of us, and everything on this physical plane.

We are one! Energy beings are aged by the many physical planes which they have experienced!

Energy beings enter this physical realm over and over again.

On entry, each energy being chooses other energy beings to join them on the journey. Each energy being has a role, which God and other higher vibration energy beings have carefully planned for the energy being while on the physical plane.

There is a bigger picture and before entry of the energy being, they know the plan, as well as the plans of other energy beings who have joined the energy being on this physical plane.

With each earth experience, the energy being has total control of the experience. Remember, each of us energy beings are pure loving light, and we never lose our connection to this light or God.

Our energy being becomes human in the physical being. The physical being is a very complex system, which interconnects with your energy being.

Each physical being is designed specifically for each energy being. Each physical being design is developed through universal God energy. The universe God energy feeds the physical earth plane.

When an energy being is wanting to experience the physical plane, each physical being must be able to sustain the vibrations of the physical plane. This is why the physical being takes nine months to develop within another physical being.

The physical plane has several different vibrations, and when an energy being enters the physical plane, they go through the vibrations of outer space while coming to a lower vibration on the earth plane. That's why each energy being has a unique vibration within their physical being. It is the journey to the entry to the earth plane that plays a significant role on our energy being's experience.

All humans are equal within their physical being. It is the energy being vibration that we carry which is different.

You may finally realize, as Kerri did, that each one of you went through a lot of different planes to reach the physical plane.

All energy beings are multidimensional. Being in the physical being is just one plane which surrounds your energy being for this one experience.

Humans talk about awakening to remembering who they are: you never lose who you are. There is nothing to remember. You are still the same energy being of pure love light that entered the earth plane.

It's your energy being who needs to learn how to function in a physical being, with the different energy vibrations on this earth plane.

God designed both beings to work together but your physical being arrives ready to enter and live on the earth plane.

It's your energy being that comes from a high vibration to a lower vibration and must learn to adjust to the different vibration of your physical being.

Once the energy being has developed her or his physical being, the journey begins. The energy being gets to know the physical being. All energy beings start out as babies, because the energy being needs to get used to the new vibrations. And as a baby grows, your energy being grows, with the baby your physical being.

A Complex Design

The physical being is a complex design for each individual energy being, which is designed through the use of two other energy beings' physical beings' bodies.

Humans call them their parents. Each one of these energy beings have very similar vibrations which allows the energy being to enter into the earth plane and is designed so the baby may have a safe place to enter. The physical being takes nine months to completion. Often the energy being will visit the physical being while in the womb. The energy being will communicate with other chosen energy beings while in the mother's womb. Remember, the energy being has full control. The energy being watches the physical being be developed the whole nine months (or however many months to birth).

The physical being is complex and when another physical being is growing inside another physical being, many changes have to occur. Both physical beings have to be similar vibrations for the energy being to be able to enter the physical being.

This is why humans become sick or crave different foods during pregnancy. Their physical beings are matching up with all three of the energy being's vibrations involved in this creation and birth.

Each of the energy beings' vibrations must interconnect so the baby's physical being will be developed perfectly for the energy being coming in.

If the energy being decides not to come in, the physical being dies (miscarriage, sudden infant death syndrome, when a baby does not survive). The physical being's system must be a vibrational match for this energy being to enter successfully onto the earth plane.

If death occurs the energy being has the choice to wait for another physical body, or not to incarnate.

Once the physical being is a perfect vibrational match, the energy being then has successful birth entering into the physical plane as a human.

The energy being begins adjusting to the earth plane through their physical being. Remember the physical being is a denser vibration than the energy being which lives on the inside of the physical being.

The complex physical being consist of nerves, brain, spinal cord, organs, bones, blood, water, muscles, tendons, cells, and skin holding it all together.

Your energy being connects with every part of the physical being. Each part of your physical being vibrates at different rates and this is where your energy being adapts to each different vibration, so connection can occur.

Your energy being, and your physical being's body must line up perfectly with your energy being's systems. The energy systems in your energy being are your chakras, meridians, aura and crystal grid which holds on to all your energy experiences from the different planes that your energy being has visited.

Humans understand how the physical being functions, but many don't realize your physical being's body is held together through your energy being's system.

The Beginning: The Connection

Once your energy being is connected into your physical being, there are several steps that must be taken to have a successful entry. When your energy being enters into the physical being and everything lines up perfectly, your energy being begins anchoring into the physical being through the legs. It's like you are getting dressed, putting on your physical being. Your energy being goes down each leg and pulls the physical being up over the abdomen and puts each arm down the sleeves of the physical being. Then it pulls the physical being up onto the shoulders then ending over top of the head.

Once the physical being's body is covering your energy being this is when the connecting begins. The first parts that your energy being connects is your eyes, nose, mouth and ears. These are the most important connections so your physical being, and energy being can communicate. In your physical being, humans can see where the eyes, nose, mouth and ears are located.

Once the physical being is totally covering your energy being you can feel were the eye, nose, mouth and ears can be felt by means of dents or holes just under the physical being's flesh.

Humans are very intuitive because of the two beings coming together. The physical being can tap into the dense vibrations and the energy being can still tap into the higher vibrations.

God created these two beings' systems to protect each other.

The energy being has one eye. This eye is located one inch above your eyebrows, in the middle. When you touch this spot, you should feel the dent and when you close your eyes you can see one eye. Humans know this as the third eye.

Your energy being's nose is located a finger below your eyebrows, on the bridge of your physical nose, you will feel a little dent. This is where your physical being can smell invisible smells.

Your energy being's mouth is located inside your physical being's mouth. Take your tongue to the back of the top of your mouth where its soft and put the tip of your tongue in that dent. It will be squishy in the dent. This is where your physical being can taste unseen taste.

Your energy being's ears are located behind your physical being's ear lobes. There is a dent at the bottom of the bone which runs along behind your ear. Each physical being ear has an energy being ear as well. These ears help the physical being to hear your energy being for guidance.

After all your communication parts are connected, your energy being moves down your body, connecting the energy systems to your physical being. Your energy being begins to connect each chakra with the physical being's different systems.

Energy being's system "Chakras and Auras"

Your energy being's system that connects to your physical being are called the chakras. Each chakra energy center feeds one or several of the 12 organ systems and surrounding area located in your physical being's body. Each chakra has a different vibration which is a perfect match to your physical being's body parts. Each human has seven main chakras feeding their physical being's physical parts.

Another energy system is called the aura, which has layers that bring in new energy vibrations. The aura also holds on to old vibrations from other life experiences.

The energy being's aura feeds the chakras and the chakras feed the physical being's physical parts.

Energy being's Meridians

Your energy meridians connect to your energy being through the nerves and lymphatic systems of the physical being. The meridians bring in energy to the nerves and lymphatic systems which run from the physical being's head to feet.

The meridians communicate from your energy being and send information to the physical being's brain which communicates to the physical being's body.

Your energy being never loses communication with the physical being. However, the energy being steps back once the physical being is up and running on its own.

Humans are visual, so close your eyes. And picture your physical being inside a balloon and the outside of the balloon holds everything together. This outside of the balloon is called your personal energy crystal grid, which keeps your energy being connected to larger crystal grid that surrounds everyone and everything God has ever created.

The crystal grid is an outer shell, which surrounds your aura about two feet. This crystal grid connects all energy being together as one. This grid holds all energy being in the proper vibration needed for each plane they visit. Your crystal grid gives the aura new vibrations of information to feed the chakras which feeds the physical being's body.

Do not get confused between your energy systems and your energy being. Your energy systems are a part of your energy being, just like your digestive system is a part of your physical being. Each energy system and physical system overlaps each other perfectly. Your energy being, and energy systems were the foundation of the design and development of your physical being.

Your crystal grid cannot be penetrated by anything on this physical plane. Your crystal grid is known by humans as your akashic records. Your crystal grid is all your energy vibrations connected to your energy being. This grid keeps your physical being and energy being connected to all the multi-dimensional planes.

The earth has energy systems as well. That is why when a human error causes the earth energy system to break down that earth doesn't dissolve. The crystal grid holds earth all together as one whole piece.

When humans think of the animals living in nature, animals also have energy systems and this crystal grid to keep them connected. The crystal grid connects everything and everyone to the universal God energy which we energy beings never lose or forget.

As this information is shown, as you begin to have clarity around humans being comprised of energy beings.

Everything is Energy

Universal God energy began developing the physical plane many years ago. God's universal energy also created other galaxies, where many energy beings were first created.

Kerri and other humans are beginning to understand those places are home planets. Every energy being is a part of God universal energy. Humans are beginning to see evidence of other life on this physical plane which doesn't belong here. Humans are trying to remember who they are, but humans are not lost. All humans need to understand that your energy being is here to enjoy the physical plane in your physical being. Your energy being understands and is very intelligent as far as what your physical being needs, and how you should live on this physical plane.

God's universal energy created beauty all around us, because humans don't understand their purpose of this experience, they are letting their physical being run their experience here on earth.

Humans understand that when living in the head takes them out of their heart. The human physical being cannot be in two places at one time. Your energy being can be in more places than one because it vibrates much higher.

After your energy being becomes comfortable with its new body, your energy being steps back and lets the physical systems take over. So, your energy being is now in the back seat observing your physical being. As the physical being grows, your energy systems begin to really connect with the physical systems.

For example, each chakra feeds an organ system. As babies, these organ systems are tiny and only need small amounts of energy. The complex energy system of your energy being regulates how much and when the physical bodies need energy.

Your physical being receives energy through several different ways from your energy being's system. Here is one way that your physical body receives from your energy system. First, after the physical being is up and functioning at full speed and all systems are connect properly, the aura begins to receive energy from God's universal energy.

Then the aura sends this energy down several layers of the aura to the chakras, which feeds the organs and areas. These energies feed around and through the physical being. This energy is also received from above and below through the meridians which feeds the physical being from head to toe. So, if you put your physical being's body inside a balloon, your physical being would receive energy from every direction. Your energy system has been designed and developed to feed your entire physical being.

When your energy being is convinced all systems are connected from your energy systems and physical systems are up and running, it lets go of the control.

As babies, our energy being is fine tuning all systems to let this human physical being take control over your energy being's future.

Now the physical experience on this earth plane begins.

Humans are here to learn and have a human experience. Humans don't need to awaken, they need education on their energy being located within their physical being.

When we remove the physical being, we become energy beings again back into our unique vibration. Humans don't feel these vibrations while in the physical being due to that there are several different vibrations needed to be housed in a physical plane.

Purpose

What is an energy being's purpose to come to a physical plane? Humans are always growing and expanding, and this is the same for energy beings. Human's purpose is to grow in understanding and develop wisdom during their physical experience.

The energy being's purpose is to get the human's physical experience to strengthen the bond of two different beings coming together and becoming one of pure love light!

Energy beings come together on the physical plane to help each other on their journey of becoming one. Many of the energy beings you have chosen to join you will be a part of the bigger plan, but your physical being generally will have no idea of the plan

Human Family

Your human family will take over caring for you after birth. Your human family will play an important role in your human development and experience. Human families don't have a rule book, so many teachings come from the family experiences.

Human families have similar vibrations. This is the attraction to the life experience required for your energy being to teach your physical being's mind and body to become one.

Becoming one in mind and spirit is the reason all of us energy beings continue journey to other planes. Success comes from learning to Become One within the physical being and energy being. This is the purpose of all energy beings and humans. Once humans understand that getting to know yourself inside and out, and once you believe and trust what your energy being is communicating, you have become whole.

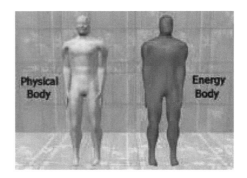

Humans must understand that they have two parts. One is the true self "energy being" and one is the "physical being."

These beings have been assigned from God to work hand in hand to help each become one. Energy beings become humans to learn to grow and vibrate in the environment which the physical being chooses. When the energy being connects to a low vibrating physical being and they become one that's when the journey begins on fulfilling the bigger plan here on earth.

This is the journey that the physical being has chosen as part of the design from mother earth. Humans walk on earth and their energy feeds mother earth through their physical feet.

Within the physical being, the energy system which helps connect humans to mother earth is described as the meridians. The meridians are the energy system which connects to the crystal grid of mother earth. Mother earth is fed through the vibrations from humans.

The crystal grid is God's net to keep everything together. God is the designer of this grid, so no human is left out or floats away. All energy beings are a part of the universal system. All energy being are the same vibrations in God's universal energy. When an energy being decides to journey to earth, that's when God and spirit counsel come together and design the perfect vibration for that energy being.

The vibrations I speak about come from all the earth experiences that energy being have been involved in for many, many planetary life times. Humans speak of these vibrations as akashic records. These vibrations are located all around the physical being when on their journey to earth. These akashic records, as humans know them, are set aside when the energy being returns to God's universal energy.

God's universal energy is pure white love light. When the energy being is in God's realm there is no need for such vibrations. It is only when the energy being chooses to leave God's universal energy that the vibrations surround the physical being again.

These akashic records play an important role in the physical being's journey. Humans understand past lives. In vibration terms, past lives are always connected to the energy being. When each energy being returns to a new planetary experience, the akashic records become a part of them again.

Once the energy being leaves God's vibration – which is the highest vibration of them all, the energy being comes down a vibration and receives their "coat" which holds the blueprint for this planetary visit.

I speak of it as a coat, so humans can understand that they have many coats, just like layers. Think of a coat as a lifetime. Each coat has experiences that have been fulfilled and some experiences which need to be fulfilled. Each coat holds onto vibrations like memories which belong to the energy being.

Each energy being has other energy beings in their vibrations, stored in their coat from previous and future journeys, but only when the energy being is not in God's vibration.

Vibrations in terms of Human Brainwaves

To clarify the different vibrations so humans can understand as human brain waves. Humans have five brain waves: beta, alpha, theta, delta and gamma. Each brainwave has its own unique vibration. Each human, while in their physical being uses these brainwaves. Each brainwave has a specific purpose within the physical being. Each brainwave feeds the physical being information to help the physical being's body to function.

These brain waves cannot be seen, but humans understand that they are there, and that is what keeps them alive. These brain waves work with no effort because they are energetically connected to your energy being's systems

The brainwave I would like to speak about is the gamma brainwave. Humans are just starting to understand gamma brainwaves. The gamma brainwave is the purest and fastest vibration that is connected to your energy being. Humans are now realizing that gamma brainwaves are a miracle tool. That by tapping into gamma brainwaves, you can heighten performance without altering your waking state. Whereas tapping into the other brainwaves, you have to go into a relax state.

But what humans don't understand is that gamma brainwaves are their connection to God. This brainwave cannot be broken down or changed. Gamma brainwaves are your energy being's golden cord connection to God's universal energy. This is why energy being always have the control.

I am going to paint you a picture. First, close your eyes, then in your mind's eye picture you. Once you see you, picture energy coming from above you. Then picture the energy above coming down through the top of your head. This energy has a bluish hue in color and is vibrating very fast down into your head. Once you see this energy coming into your physical being through the head, you have succeeded in tapping into your gamma brainwaves. It is very simple to tap into all the brainwaves in the physical realm.

Energy beings have only one purpose while on this planetary visit and that is to understand the physical being and be able to integrate both the physical being and energy being together in love and light.

Effects of Energy

In this picture there are three spots where white energy is coming into and around the physical being and is coming from the universe and the human's world.

To interconnect the energy being to the physical being while in human form, the physical being must be able to receive and give unconditional love energy from their energy being.

In human terms, the three spots as illustrated on the image are the crown chakra, the third eye chakra, and heart. The physical being is always receiving energy messages through their gamma brainwaves. This is the only way humans can tap into a high vibration energy without losing their coat.

Helping Others

Humans love to help others. I watched Kerri help many other physical beings, which helps Kerri grow closer to her own energy being. Kerri's trial and error has led to many different energy vibrations which attached to her coat.

Through Kerri's experiences she now understands the effects vibrations have on the physical being's body. Humans must understand this planetary visit is for themselves. There is nobody else in the picture or blocking or receiving the white energy from above or in front of the physical being.

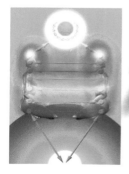

Here is a picture I created to show humans how their energy connects between each other. The first picture you can see two humans sitting looking at each other. The coat I spoke about is what humans know as aura and chakras. Each physical being has their own coat which surrounds them at all times. If I was to compare children to adults: the first would be two children and the second picture would be two adults because children don't often carry heavy dense energy until adulthood. Because children are active their energy replenishes often throughout their physical being.

Human children arrive on to earth bright and colorful and still connected to their energy being. When adults look into a baby's eyes and say they are old souls, that is because their energy being is still in control for the first to second year. That's when children begin to walk and talk and can control their physical being. This baby stage of your the physical being is your energy being anchoring into your physical being's body. This stage is where the energy being's systems interconnect with the physical systems of the physical body.

Here is a picture to show the energy being's coat surrounding the physical being and being held together by the energy systems and crystal grid.

Every energy being and physical being begins at the same spot as babies. Even though this picture shows an adult physical form in your mind's eye, picture a baby. While the physical being needs a tiny the coat, the energy being's coat remains the same size. As the baby grows into an adult, the oversize energy system begins to fit like it's supposed to fit.

When the energy being enters into the stage as the human baby, both the energy being's and physical being must connect through energy vibrations and gamma brainwaves before this connection can be anchor into the physical body.

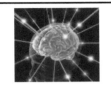 

Once this connection from the energy being and physical being has been completed the other energy systems begin to connect to the physical being. Humans must understand it is their energy systems which keeps the physical being alive. Without the energy being, the physical being would just die. Life comes from energy as humans knows it as "chi energy" but this is God's energy.

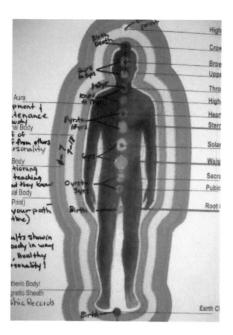

As the energy being and physical being interconnect their systems each energy system attaches to the physical body at different vibrations and different times and human ages. The physical being grows at different rates into their energy coat or energy systems.

Humans learn that the body runs by itself, but this is not true. God designed the physical being to come alive when the energy being enters into the physical being's body. It takes a very complex system to integrate each being to become one.

The picture shows the energy systems chakras and auras around and through the physical body. Each energy system was developed to feed other parts of the energy systems and keep each area of the physical being's body alive and functional at optimal health.

Each one of these energy systems comes with an intelligence of knowing what is best for that physical system in that location of the physical being's body.

The energy being doesn't relate to time or birthdays. The energy being is an intelligent creation which can move around and has no limits. The physical being is trained to experience time and birthdays throughout their journey of the earth plane.

Organ Systems

The physical being has 12 major organ systems which play an important role in keeping the physical being's body in optimal health.

Each chakra has a color for energy centers as chakras and spin like a wheel. God created these colorful energy centers in the energy being so the connection to the physical being's body would be simple for humans to remember. The development of the colors of each energy center offers a different vibration.

The chakra colors were developed in relationship to the speed of the energy needed for the physical being's body systems.

These energy centres were designed by God as a system to receive and give colour coded energy to the chakras, which feed the physical body systems. Each energy center, or "chakra" has only one job: to send energy and receive energy, that is it.

Each energy center flows through the front of the physical body and connects to the aura, flows to the back of the physical body and connects to the aura, up to the chakra above and connects to the chakra, and down to the chakra below and connects with that chakra.

While the colored energy centers are flowing through the physical being the physical body is being fed new energy.

The energy being begins feeding the physical body from first entry into the physical body. The physical body develops at different rates and your energy being continues to feed and fill the physical body until the energy centers are running at full capacity.

It's like when you are in your mother's womb, she feeds you until you are fully ready to enter this world, then you are born.

Your energy being is like your mother. It continues to feed your energy centers until the physical being is totally connected to your physical body systems. In which your physical being can transfer of color energy from the other energy systems on its own.

Before the energy being steps back and allows the physical being to take control, the aura and chakra systems must be transferring proper vibration color energy to each physical body system and surrounding areas.

In the beginning when the energy being enters the physical being's body through the head and the connection to mother earth is created. In this picture the red-looking branches that run down each leg is how your energy being anchors to mother earth.

Humans know this as the root chakra and is known as the color red. The root chakra feeds red energy to the female and male parts which are the circulatory systems and the bladder, for proper growth and functioning.

The energy being's job is to connect an energetic cord to the physical being's body through all the energy centers from head to feet. The energetic cord which runs through the physical being attaches two feet above the physical head and two feet below the physical feet, which connects to the crystal grid. The energy being's systems are part of crystal grid and is connected throughout the physical being's body. In this connection process the crystal grid interconnects with the meridians, aura and chakras. The energy being's energy is strong within the crystal grid and weakens as it enters into the physical being's body.

This is the coat I spoke about that holds all the energy being's experiences, as well as the physical being blue print. Look at the picture above, the coat is everything that surrounds your physical being.

The root chakra refers to the red branches running down the legs in the picture and anchors into the earth chakra below the physical feet. Once the energy being anchors in the physical being at the head and through the feet the crystal grid automatically becomes connected. This is why humans don't float away. The root chakra is connected to circulatory system in the physical body.

The circulatory system receives energy from the meridians which comes from the energy aura around the physical being. Remember the meridians run from head to feet and feet to head. The meridians only feed the physical body in these directions. The meridians are a part of the crystal grid that runs through the physical being's body.

{At this time if the energy being decides the physical body isn't perfect this is the time most often the energy being will let the physical being go. If the energy being is satisfied with the physical body, then the physical being and energy being interconnection continues.}

The second chakra that the energy being fills is the sacral chakra and its energy color is orange. This second chakra feeds orange energy to the human's small and large intestines.

The third chakra your energy being fills is your solar plexus and its energy color is yellow. This chakra feeds yellow energy to the human systems of the stomach, liver, gallbladder, kidneys, spleen and pancreas.

The fourth chakra the energy being fills is the heart chakra. This chakra is green-colored energy and feeds the heart. The heart chakra and feeds green energy to the heart and lungs.

The fifth chakra is the throat chakra and its energy color is blue. The throat chakra feeds blue energy to the thyroid.

The sixth chakra is the brow or third eye chakra and its energy color is indigo. The brow chakra feeds blue energy to the brain.

The seventh chakra is the crown chakra and its color is white, which is how the energy being enters into the physical being's body. The crown chakra receives universal energy filled with wisdom from God to send to the rest of the physical body.

The energy being takes these seven colored energy centers and connects them with the twelve body systems, while the body is in the mother's womb. When you are born, they slap your butt, and all connections of the energy being and physical being's body start working all at once after you take that first breath. It is like putting gas in your car. Once the energy is flowing the correct rate for your physical being body to survive, the energy being steps back.

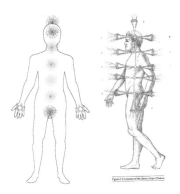

In these pictures you can see the colors. You can see where each color is located and see how each direction the energy at the chakras flows in the physical body.

When two people sit across from each other this is what the chakras and aura should look like.

All energy beings are pure colored light. But humans are not taught about the energy centers that keep them alive.

Humans understand oxygen from the air keeps them alive by breathing in oxygen through the nose or mouth into the lungs. The lungs then take the oxygen and feed the physical body. All true! Oxygen in my language is energy. Where does energy come from? Where does oxygen come from? The exact same place: the universe.

Oxygen and energy are all around humans. Oxygen and energy are the exact same thing. Oxygen and energy are needed to keep the physical being alive.

If the oxygen quits the body dies. If the energy stops flowing the physical being's body dies slowly.

The picture shows a healthy energy system and a unhealthy energy system.

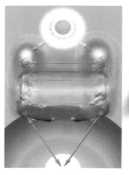

Here the same two people sitting in front of each other, but the healthy colored energy is not so healthy now. Why?

The first picture is when humans first meet and their vibrations match both are in a lighter vibration. This vibration Is connected to words or thoughts like love, happy, joy. Each of these thoughts feeds the physical beings mind with light vibrations. Each physical being feeds each other colorful energy vibrations.

For example, when Kerri met her helper the energy transferring between them was light and bright. But over time their energy transfer became darker like the second picture.

Kerri's Story

When humans choose other physical beings to join them on this earth experience, there are stepping stones involved.

The other physical being steps into the role and vibration. In Kerri's case the role of her helper was an abuser with a dark dense vibration of physical and mental abuse.

Kerri's energy being had stepped back and the physical being was functioning correctly with physical systems before meeting this physical being.

Kerri has already programmed her brain from previous experiences from her human family.

When your physical being begins on the journey each experience becomes a layer. Humans need to understand putting on the layers is very similar to your energy being entering your physical being. Think of these layers as your physical being's coat which are the experiences that your physical being has gone through. Remember the purpose of the energy being is to house your energy being.

Humans aren't educated on their energy being's purpose. So, each layer is a stepping stone on the journey which physical being has completed or still going through.

When the two physical beings come together their vibrations must interconnect. So, Kerri and her helper needed to connect for the relationship could take place.

When Kerri's physical being began connecting with the other being his energy it was much denser than Kerri's, but the connection took place still.

In the beginning these two beings were a good vibrational match, but once the abuse began the vibration changed.

His vibration changed when he abused Kerri. And Kerri's vibration changed when she gave into him. Over time Kerri started believing his words. This is when his dark dense vibration was feeding both physical being's bodies.

Kerri was putting his vibration on like a coat, just like putting on her energy being coat on her physical being. Because Kerri liked this man and she believed him that he loved her. She started thinking more about him which anchored his vibration throughout her mind and then her heart and then the rest of her physical being. Kerri at the time didn't realize this was happening to her. This is how humans become comfortable in unhealthy situations. Many humans in abusive situation don't realize the abuser has them in an energy prison where the abuser is in control. The human victim believes this control because once the energy of the abuser connects with the victim's physical being it's like being tied up. Humans give such behaviours other names such as codependent or addicted, but it's neither. Other physical being's aren't programmed to be in others physical's vibration. There no name needed just an understanding about your own unique vibrations!

When humans have another physical being's energy within their physical being's body this means both vibrations are feeding the organs of the body.

"Remember your physical being's body was only designed for your energy being's energy not others energy."

When your physical being is filled with others energy it can't receive or give the proper messages to the mind or body. Which makes all your systems run with others physical being's vibration of energy. Humans, it's like mixing two different gases in your car and the engine systems get confused and won't start.

Humans realize that if you don't add the proper gas to your car the car doesn't run! It is the same with your physical and energy systems. If you stop feeding the physical being's systems colorful light energy, the physical being's coat becomes cluttered. This turns the colorful energy into dark energy resulting in body aches, pains, sickness, depression, anxiety, disease the list goes on.

If the doctor can't find anything wrong in your physical being's body, it's because it's not in your body but in your energy systems.

Your energy being has the wisdom to remove toxic vibrations and heal your physical being's body.

Kerri was taught this through the lump in her breast. The doctor removed the lump, but another lump showed up in the same breast two months later.

This lump Kerri removed on her own without a doctor. Kerri learned that the lump was in her lymphatic system. By learning about the lymphatic system Kerri, was able to remove the blockage "lump" by using energy to move it out.

Kerri's lessons were given by her energy being, so she would understand the importance of movement of energy.

Why does this occur in such a perfect system from God?

When other physical being's energy enters into another's physical being's body and the physical beings body begins to break down. This is the beginning of God's plan to becoming one.

Humans aren't educated on their energy systems that the physical beings body needs to survive.

Kerri's experiences of healing herself through connecting with her energy being has given her the knowledge to see beyond her physical being's body into her energy systems. Kerri has done the work through the help of the spiritual plane.

Kerri knows the systems break down when it's time to become one. When these systems become overloaded with dense energy, the colorful light energy can't feed the physical body systems like in the beginning. Each human only finds healing through themselves.

How do the physical systems become dense dark energy?

Dense dark energy happens when the human does not care for the physical being's body properly, which their energy being designed for them. Over several years Kerri's physical being was totally dark from receiving dark energy from her helper through the abuse.

The energy vibration in the design becomes lost in other unwanted vibrations. The energy colors get mixed and confused on the rate of vibrations when feeding the physical being. So, the chakras end up not knowing their jobs because of other physical being energy inside the physical being's body. The organs and surrounding areas don't receive the proper energy to keep them functioning at optimal health.

When this happens, the physical being begins to talk to the human responsible for the up keep. The physical being begins to talk through aches and pains. If the physical being isn't taken seriously, the physical being speaks louder by becoming sick. Kerri's physical being was sick throughout this human relationship.

If the human still doesn't listen, the physical being will just shut down where the human can't do anything but listen. Then the physical being can communicate the issues with the human. Most humans resort to doctors, and after that is unsuccessful the humans start looking other places.

Kerri started with readings books just like this one. One book taught her to meditate and ask God to come into her heart. Kerri sat for hours waiting for a response from God. That is when her energy being was introduced to Kerri and her guide, me, "Mel". It was from this moment Kerri's energy being and I "Mel" started to form a relationship. Kerri believed she was talking to God.

Kerri was so hungry to change she was very open to hearing from me each day. She absorbed everything her energy being told her. Kerri's energy being has never left her. But now her energy being was able to come back into the play because she did the work of releasing the layers, she gathered from the abuse experience.

Her energy being was becoming an important part of her life and she knew she it was her energy being helping her get healthier and stronger, when her helper was gone.

Kerri tapping into her energy being has given her control to live the life she deserves.

Kerri understands and believes that her energy being kept her alive during the physical and mental abuse. Her physical being stopped functioning correctly from the dense dark energy from others.

"When human's starts looking for answers in other places, this is the beginning of the physical being and energy being finding each other again. This journey of understanding what's wrong with your physical being's body is when humans learn what is good and not good for their physical beings. This is the stage God waits for because he knows when this stage begins, the human will need lots of spiritual support."

The part God loves is that humans can only heal by going inside of their physical being. The outside world no longer has the control over the human because the outside world couldn't answer or help heal the physical being's body.

God's plan is that all humans become lost and return to him for true healing which comes through knowing your energy being.

www.kpcsphotography.com

Kerri's earthly plane experience of learning to become one began in a human family where there was physical and mental abuse. Her energy being knows the bigger plan, but the physical being does not. Kerri chose this experience to learn from it and to become one.

Kerri changing her energy thoughts and creating weight loss within her physical being connected her to her energy being. This taught and showed her colorful energy vibrations of acceptance, self-love, and self-worth. Each energy being is perfect, but to become one within each other the human must go through dysfunction to find the real energy being which lies within their physical being!

Once you realize your energy thoughts are your weight loss pill, your life will continue to be as you see it.

Conclusion

Energy is all around us before we are born and as we grow up our energy grows with us.

Human family plays an important role in feeding you the information to get you prepared for the world. Attending school, college or university prepares you for the future. After you move out on your own you have completed this part of the requirements.

Over time as adults our home life teachings begins to show up in our life, we have created for ourselves. In Kerri's case the mental abuse started taking a toll on her physical body and mind. Her thoughts went from happy-go-lucky to dark mean self-talk.

His words Kerri repeated in her head, which she programed her physical body to be. This all reflected what she told herself.

Kerri ended up becoming fat and very unhealthy. When the physical abuse began, her physical body was already programed from her own thoughts, then the hitting confirmed that she deserved the treatment.

Over the years of being in the same unhealthy environment, Kerri became accustomed to the unhealthy energy vibration from the mental and physical abuse.

When Kerri's energy being first started communicating with her, the voice was very loud and authoritarian. For example, Kerri was planning on leaving after her helper was gone to work, but over the next couple hours the tension settled down and Kerri was going to stay. But when her helper left, Kerri's energy being demanded she leave and not look back.

That night she went to a friend's house to hide out. The first day at her friends, house Kerri got a message to remove her car from the yard. So, Kerri put her car out in the middle of the cow pasture. The second night Kerri was there, the man came to the house during the night while everyone was sleeping. Kerri's energy being woke her up to make her aware he was there, but her energy being made her feel safe.

Kerri went to her friend's room and sat in the closet with her two dogs. Her friend's dog just looked at her but never barked. After about ten minutes, the man left, and Kerri's energy being told her "OK, it's safe to go back to bed."

Kerri always wondered how he found her. It's simple to explain. Kerri's physical being was full of the abuser's energy vibrations. That unhealthy energy from the environment from the abuse become imprinted into Kerri's physical being. Like when you think of someone, they show up or call, same idea.

As Kerri thought of him and he drove around looking for her he could feel her vibration. He got close but didn't find her because she was in her friend's closet. Plus, the other physical being's vibration on the farm confused his own vibration so he made his mind up that she was not there.

This energy imprinting is when a place or person becomes filled up with energy. In Kerri's case, the abusive energy surrounded her in her home all day every day. Her physical being breathed that dark dense energy.

To help you human's understand Kerri's situation, we are going to look at energy as oxygen. Every day Kerri's physical being was living in unhealthy oxygen. Kerri's physical being received from the trauma vibration from the abuser. This lived in every cell of her physical being. Kerri never went to the doctor, so she never knew how sick her helper was making her by living this dark dense unhealthy energy.

It was when Kerri visited a psychic she got confirmation that her environment and her helper was the cause of her physical being's body being depressed, overweight, anxiety and the lump in her breast.

You humans all have stories. We are using Kerri's story to show how human choices cause the physical being's body to become overweight from others' vibrations.

Over time Kerri's physical being became over-weight and Kerri felt 10x's bigger. Kerri did all kinds of diets, pills, exercise and meditating but nothing help her long term. They were all short lived.

Kerri's physical being was filled up with unhealthy energy/ oxygen throughout. Her physical being's body couldn't get healthy enough to heal itself. The reason why Kerri's physical being couldn't heal itself was because Kerri never knew anything about vibrations that were causing her body not to function well.

Kerri knew she was being hurt by this man, but she didn't realize the extent damage of her physical being. All human's get all kinds of signs that their physical being's body is in crisis, but many humans are only taught through doctors. Kerri never went to the doctor. Her energy being guided her and what she learned from her parents, to fix her own physical being.

Kerri's physical being's body was in perfect alignment when she entered into her relationship with her helper.

Kerri put her helper first before her own health. Over time through the abuse Kerri could see that he was not a good vibrational match anymore.

But why couldn't she leave him?

When humans live in an environment over a long time, the physical being becomes used to that energy and change is hard.

Kerri's whole physical being was already pro-gramed to take the abuse from her family. Her energy systems were already overloaded with family dysfunction. When children are sick as children, it's the environment they live in making them sick.

Her children were living in abusive energy. She understands how her body was fed dark energy instead of colorful energy during the abusive days. But she could leave or would leave but return several times.

Energy weight loss changed her life. She began to understand when she removed other's energy from her body, she lost weight and gained control.

We are already dense energy, and when we carry other people's energy, we become very heavy.

Our physical body can't function properly because heavy energy is not in God's plan. The physical body is very strong and will carry you, but it will kick and scream through aches, pains, sickness or disease to get your attention. The physical body will put up with this heavy energy until it reaches your energy being which only knows love light energy.

When you aren't well, both your physical being and energy being are no longer a vibrational match. Change has to occur, or this is when the physical being begins to die slowly. Kerri is so grateful for the lumps in her breasts, for this she began the journey of becoming one with herself.

For energy weight loss, it is very important to understand that losing dense energy with in your physical being is how you change your life.

Kerri couldn't understand for the longest time why she kept going back to that lifestyle. It was the dense energy that was accumulated which was located throughout her entire physical being.

Leaving fed Kerri physical being's body new energy but not enough to change her lifestyle. It was when Kerri started to learn and focus on learning and clearing her energy systems that Kerri could get strong enough to leave that lifestyle. As you humans remove other vibrations that no longer match your vibration that's when you can't receive messages from the spirit realm.

Kerri was getting sick at certain times of the year. When she did see doctors, they couldn't figure out what was wrong with her but all the time her physical being was telling her that her original vibrations were out of alignment.

In contrast, understanding energy and how it can heal your physical being, allows you not to attach the dense energies that once harmed you. After Kerri learning about her physical being's body and her energy systems, she now can feel unhealthy dense energies attaching to her physical being body, before they can harm her. She is still on the energy weight loss plan and she is healthy.

They are many tools out there to help clear your energy but until you do your own work on clearing you the tools are just bandages.

It was when Kerri went inside of herself where she was crying alone that changes began occurring. God showed Kerri the real Kerri, how beautiful she was. Removing the layers from the physical being coat has taught her the truth about the purpose we are here on earth. This truth has gotten her to love herself more each day.

Our physical being was designed to only carry our own vibrational energy. Getting back to our perfect weight of our energy that feds our physical being is how we remove the dense energy.

Energy and weight loss is the key to you changing and living a healthy abundant life!

All humans have opportunities to learn and heal their own physical beings just like Kerri experienced.

Kerri's journey of energy and weight loss has given her the insight to how to help others in their own journey of energy weight loss.

Understand, you are an energy being here on this earth plane to have a human experience. During this experience, learning about your own energy and understanding you can heal your own physical being is part of the whole plan.

Each stepping stone is an experience which gets you closer to discovering the real you!

The different energy systems and different physical systems when brought together will give humans the way to overcome any adversity that they go through.

The physical being must educate themselves on the unseen energies. Then they can begin to see and believe there are much more than humans in this earth plane experience.

It is only the human who can change the dense energy within their physical being's body, no one else.

The physical being is not alone and by going within they will find that loss piece which was never lost again. The energy being which is the real you, the perfect you, is one with you.

Becoming one with your energy being and physical being is every human's purpose for this earth plane experience.

Knowledge is wisdom and practicing is freedom!

THE END

www.kerri-the buttonlady.com

CPSIA information can be obtained
at www.ICGtesting.com
Printed in the USA
BVHW020230230419
546247BV00001B/1/P